Understanding and Interpreting

DREAMS

BRIAN MGABAZI

Copyright © 2020 Brian Mgabazi

First edition April 2013

Printed in Harare, Zimbabwe

ISBN: 978-1-77925-294-4

DEDICATION

This book is dedicated to the Holy Spirit, to my dear wife Blessing our children whom I love dearly. Girls, you are my world, my love and my life. May the good Lord continue to guide you, so that you may walk in greatness, in power, and love?

CONTENTS

ACKNOWLEDGMENTS

Many people have supported and with me as I wrote this book. Some have helped in editing and getting this book published. I would like to thank Covenant Life Ministries International for standing with me, and all my friends for the unwavering prayer and support

1

ORIGINS OF DREAMS

INTRODUCTION

Understanding dreams and their origins

I once had a dream. In the dream I stood beside a river, wearing a fur coat. The place was very cold. Behind me, there was a building. I asked people around to tell me where we were? A man said, "We are in Estonia." I then asked what was written on the building and he said to me: "It says Brian Mgabazi Proprietor".

When I woke up, I couldn't understand what the dream meant. I searched on the atlas for Estonia. There was none. The vividness of the dream could not be easily erased from my mind that day. It was just so real. I could not erase the nostalgia around me as I thought of this dream. The problem was I could not understand the dream but I knew it meant something. I wished to understand what it meant. I could not interpret what the dream meant and what was being communicated to me through that dream.

Years later in 1999, the nation of Estonia was established out of the former Union Soviet Socialist Republic (USSR). It was amazing that I had seen the nation about three years earlier on, before its birth. From that moment I began to realize that God speaks through dreams. God has a way of communicating His message to His people through dreams.

Later on, it was put upon my heart to write a book on dreams. I had to help many people, including myself who missed out on what God is saying and failing to find direction in life because they cannot deduce what God is saying to them through their dreams. I have taught on this subject many times in our Church.

I pray and hope that after reading through this book, you will also believe and change your perspective on dreams. This is probably a very contentious and often misunderstood subject worldwide. There is a psychological perception of dreams and a spiritual viewpoint on this subject. According to the Oxford dictionary, a dream is "a series of pictures of events in a sleeping person's mind. A dream is an ambition or ideal to dream up-to imagine, to invent".

This interpretation is pregnant with validation. The questions that arise are: where are these pictures and events coming from? I have put down explanations of what dreams can be viewed as.

Dreams are a glance by the human spirit into the unseen realms, as she/he gazes into the past, present and future. A human being is not just flesh: she/he is spirit, soul and body. When a person is asleep, his/her body is sleeping but the spirit man is alive and awake and he can travel to see the present, past and future. The spirit of men is always alert. The spirit lives beyond the natural and can gaze into the unseen and unnatural world, bringing the pictures into reality.

Many people see events before they happen. This is what has been coined as de javu. You can get to a place and see the events as they unfold before you realize that you have experienced it before. Dreams tend to show you the future and reveal to you things before they happen.

Secondly, dreams are the voice of God to his children to give them warnings and show them what will be coming in the future. God has used dreams from time immemorial to communicate and send messages. The book of Job gives us a good explanation which is the basis upon which this book is all based on

"For God speaks once, yes twice, yet man perceives it not. In a dream in a prophetic vision of the night when deep sleep falls upon men as they slumber on their beds then He opens the ears of men seal their ears with instruction." – Job 33:14

Many dreamers were shown the future by God through dreams in the bible. Men like Abraham saw the future of Israel in Egypt. Pharaoh was able to see the famine that would come and it was done through a dream. Usually, nothing happens to us without God having revealed it. There is a part of us that gets the warning of impending challenges and problems that we often choose to ignore.

Dreams are an encouragement and point to the future.

"And when Gideon was coming, behold there was a man that told a dream unto his fellow and said Behold I dreamed a dream and I saw a cake of barley bread tumbled into the host of Midian and came unto a tent, and then it fell and overturned it that the tent lay along and his fellow answered and said This is nothing else save the sword of Gideon."
– Judges 7:13

So dreams will encourage you and show you your future. Gideon was able to see the future and all the events that would happen. The situation that he was facing was tough and discouraging but the dream he had encouraged him.

A prominent Zimbabwean businessperson, Strive

Masiyiwa says that when they went to Nigeria for a Telecoms License, he had a dream of what would happen at the License Auction. The events happened as he had seen earlier in his dream. This encouraged him and he knew the Lord was with him.

The bible is filled with men that prayed and in dreams saw what God had done for them. David prayed, "God show me my end." God was able to reveal to David what would befall him.

Dreams are an open door into the spiritual realm.

"And he dreamed, and behold a ladder set up on the earth, and top of it reached to heaven and behold the angels of God ascending and descending on it and behold the Lord stood above it and said I am the God of Abraham thy father." – Genesis 28:12

Jacob had an encounter with God. Most people want an encounter with God. And dreams are usually the easiest way in which one can encounter

God and can see visions. Most experiences with God, angels, heaven and hell have been through dreams. When God wants you to see the spiritual world; it's easier in dreams because you are not in control of your thought processes. Dreams are more spiritual than the physical reality.

Dreams are a way to get a transfer of spiritual gifts to the physical reality. Most spiritual activities and exchanges happen in the dreams. Experiencing the heavens or hell can easily happen through dreams.

"In Gibeon, the Lord appeared to Solomon in a dream by night and God said Ask what I shall give thee, but have asked for thyself understanding to discern judgment Behold, I have done according to thy words I have given thee a wisdom and understanding heart, verse. And Solomon awoke and behold it was a dream and he came to Jerusalem and stood before the ark of the covenant of the Lord and offered peace offerings. Whatever we receive or lose in a dream it comes into manifestation" – 2 Chronicles 1:7-15

Dreams also give us strategies on how to deal with diverse issues of life, business and governance. When looking for answers, dreams can easily give the solutions that someone is looking for. Many people have issues that they cannot solve but dreams offer these solutions. It's easy to get answers from dreams. A lot of inventors always talk about having dreamt of something before it manifested.

"And Pharaoh said unto Joseph I have dreamt a dream, and there is none that can interpret it; I have heard that you can interpret dreams." – Genesis 41:15

Dreams can trouble you, take away your joy, or bring you joy.

"Wherefore look you so sadly today and they said we have dreamed a dream and there is no one to interpret." – Genesis 40:6-8

Dreams are a verdict of one's future. Genesis 40 deals with the dreams of the baker and the butler.

The baker dreamt of his death, while the butler dreams of his restoration. Some dreams will seal a person's fate. There are things that once you dream of, like a sealed prophecy, they are established forever and will come to pass.

Dreams are for the mature as the scriptures in Joel says. The old men shall dream dreams as a result of the coming of the Holy Spirit. Dreams are called the gift of the Elders. This is a gift of the mature in Christ. These only come to those who can distinguish between the natural and the supernatural.

"And it shall come to pass afterwards that I will pour out my spirit upon all flesh; and your sons and daughters shall prophesy; your old man shall dream dreams; your young men shall see visions."
– Joel 2:28

"And in the second year of the reign of Nebuchadnezzar, Nebuchadnezzar dreamed a dream, wherewith his spirit was troubled and his sleep brake from him." – Daniel 2:1

Dreams are so powerful that they can change your life and your destiny and can take you up or down. How many times has God warned us in a dream? How many times has He sealed instructions in your ears and still you did not hear him? All the great people in the bible experienced across dreams, such as Joseph, Daniel, Nebuchadnezzar, Herod, Peter, and Pharaoh. God gave pharaoh a prophecy of the seven years of plenty and seven years of drought. This came through a dream.

Dreams will reveal things that are coming shortly. It's important not to take dreams for granted.

Dreams are also a transfer of spiritual reality into the physical reality. We are spiritual beings, with a temporal human experience and not human beings with a temporal spiritual experience. It's important to notice that God has made you a spirit and you have a body. You should, therefore, watch your dreams.

Dreams can get you what you want from the spirit into the natural. When you dream of receiving something it's usually very easy to receive it in the physical. Most manifestations of things in the physical started from the spiritual and it's shown through dreams.

Dreams are a conduit of transferring spiritual reality into the physical realm. There are a lot of dreams that people have that will end up manifesting into the physical. Most effects of demonic dreams, like dreams of eating and spiritual spouses, are easy to notice when one wakes up in the morning. The manifestation will happen when receive or lose things during a dream.

Dreams are the access point of taking what is not seen to bring it into the visible realm. Great men, especially inventors, talk of having dreamt of ideas at night and then brought them into physical reality. The reality is that the spiritual world communicates with us prophetically through dreams.

Many misfortunes that a lot of people face would have been experienced in the realm of dreams. We must, therefore, be very conscious of the dreams we have because they will cause us to experience a lot of things in the physical.

Limitations to accessing the Spiritual realm

It is important to understand that you cannot receive anything unless it has been released, from the spiritual realm into the natural.

"Through faith we understand that the worlds were framed by the word of God, so that the things which are seen were not made of things that do appear." – Hebrews 11: 3

Everything we possess has to be transferred out of the spiritual realm to the natural. We then have to be able to access the spiritual realm and receive what belongs to us. The limiting factor for living in the spiritual realm is our flesh. When Jesus Christ came to the earth, though He was omnipotent, omnipresent, and being God himself, He was clothed in flesh and couldn't do much. For 33 years on earth, He was limited. Though a hundred percent God and hundred percent men, He had limitations due to the flesh that He had put on. When He was crucified on the cross, He removed the flesh and unveiled Himself and there was earthquake and darkness on earth and tearing of the temple veil. Why did He unveil himself?

God Himself was coming out of the limitations of the flesh to the world. He could now do anything, including traveling in space and time; go through walls. Why? Because He is a spirit,

The flesh is the inhibiting factor for us to access the spiritual realm. The word says, *"Through faith, we understand that the world was framed by the word of God so that things which are seen were not made of things that appear, so everything is a product of the realm of the spirit."* So when we sleep, the flesh which is the inhibiting factor to access the realm of the spirit is sleeping and our spirit men can therefore maneuver and go to the next level. We fast and pray so that the flesh may die and we begin to walk in the realm of the spirit.

"In Gibeon the Lord appeared to Solomon in a dream by night and God said ask what shall I do for give thee, he says Give thy servant an understanding heart to judge thy people that I may discern between good and bad and God said I will give the riches and honor." – 1Kings 3:5

"Solomon awoke and behold it was a dream and he came to Jerusalem and stood before the ark of the covenant of the Lord, and offered up burnt offering, and peace offerings and made a feast to his entire servant." – 1Kings 3:15

Solomon only dreamt of speaking to God. Was he speaking to God really or it was just a dream? It wasn't just a dream; it was a spiritual reality. Though his body was sleeping, the men (spirit) were not asleep but having a conversation with Jehovah in the spiritual realm.

"The spirit himself bear witness with our spirit, that we are the children of God." – Roman 8:16

There is a communication channel between your spirit and God's spirit. Solomon's spirit was so strong and aware that his mind, his intellect, wisdom, emotions, thought and conscience was asleep but his spirit saw and answered God well. That's why the bible says:

"Those that are led by the spirit of God are the children of God". – Romans 8:14

Solomon dreamt and received from God in a dream and what he received became a physical reality. What about you? You can receive from God, demons, or even witches in a dream. Dreams are a very powerful medium that God will use to minister and speak to you through gifts, wealth, and all other things. God wants to give out to his childhood dreams and part of it is prophecy.

"Do not neglect the gift you have, which was given you by prophecy when the council of elders laid their hands on you." – 1Timothy 4:14

Prophecy will release gifts into your life. Job 33:14 says that dreams are a prophecy that ought to be released into our lives. Joseph dreamt himself as a governor (Prime Minister of Egypt). The baker dreamt of his death by hanging, whilst the butler dreams of his restoration. Jacob saw the open heavens and it manifested in his life.

I once met Nancy, a 28-year-old mother of two. She had separated from her husband and nothing seemed to be working in her life. She had all kinds of problems when I met her. One of her problems was a swollen finger and she was asking for prayers. I asked her what had happened. She said she had dreamt of dogs chasing her and biting her finger. When she woke up, her finger was swollen. We prayed for her and demons manifested in her. She was set free that day. The swelling suddenly subsided and there was a restoration in her marriage.

So how can her dream be so powerful to affect her in the physical?

The dream world is a real world; it's a realm on its own. Tell me how the dream world isn't connected to the spirit world? Now can you tell me how the spirit world doesn't control physical reality?

It seems whenever God had an important message to give to the world, he used dreams. Several men like Joseph, Jacob, Nebuchadnezzar, Pharaoh, Solomon, Joseph the father of Jesus, and the wise men were all dreamers. It's a very common way of receiving from the spiritual realm and seeing what is happening in the spirit. It's important to notice that the enemy intends to manipulate your dreams and steal what God has prepared for you

Dreams are the access point of taking what is not seen to bring it into the visible realm

2

MAJOR DREAMS AND DREAMERS IN THE BIBLE

Abimelech

"But God came to Abimelech in a dream by night, and said to him, "Behold, you are a dead man, for the woman whom you have taken for she is another man's wife." – Genesis 20:3

Abimelech took Sarah, Abraham's wife, and then in a dream at night, God visits Abimelech and has a conversation with him. Abimelech answers God and pleads his case before the Creator. God tends to appear to the children of men and speak to them in dreams. It is important to understand that it didn't stop in the biblical times; it's still happening today.

Jacob

"And he dreamed, and beholds a ladder set up on the earth, and the top of it reached to heaven; and behold the angels of God ascending and descending on it, and behold God stood above it, and said, "I am the Lord God of Abraham your father, in thy seed shall all the families of the earth be blessed." – Genesis 28:12

Jacob saw the Lord in a dream and his calling, blessing, and future was confirmed.

"Joseph dreamed a dream, and he told it to his brothers and they hated him the more." – Genesis 37:5

Joseph is one of the most important people in the history of the bible. His life begins with a dream. The bible says he dreamt and told his brothers the dream. This is the first mistake a lot of people make. Don't be hasty in sharing your dream with everybody. There are dream catchers and dream killers out there. Pray about it first, before you share your dream with anybody. Joseph had an interesting dream. In this dream, he was in a field harvesting and his sheaf rose above the others. The other sheaves bowed to his. In dreams, some things can represent you. The symbols that can represent you include a car, house, and any other possessions.

Joseph's brothers immediately interpreted his dream and were not happy. He had the second dream. That's why it's important to notice recurring dreams. In the second dream, the sun, moon and the stars were bowing to him. These represented his family and he could see what it meant. In the light of those dreams, his brothers plotted against him. Joseph was put in a pit, and sold to the Ishmaelite, later sold to Potiphar's and finally put in prison. In prison, he met two dreamers, a baker and a butler. They both had dreams and were troubled.

Joseph interpreted their dreams in Genesis 40. The butler dreamt a vine with three branches, and the branches blossomed and bloomed bringing forth ripe grapes. Joseph interprets that in three days, he will be restored as a butler.

The key thing to notice is the fruitfulness of the dream. Notice how the butler and the baker dreamt. It had something to do with their respective calling and mission.

The baker dreams of three baskets of bread on top of his head and birds came and ate from the baskets. The baskets represented three days and the birds represented demons that came to eat his life and future. Joseph interpreted it and it was fulfilled. Joseph came out of prison after he interpreted Pharaoh's dream. Pharaoh dreamt standing on the edge of a river and seven fat cows came out and then seven thin ones came later. The seven thin eat the seven fat ones. The cows Joseph interpret them as years. That why it's important to notice the numbers in every dream. Joseph had a life that was full of dreams and was all about dreams. So you cannot afford to take them lightly.

Prophets are also appointed in dreams.

"Now the words; if there be a prophet among you, I the Lord will make myself known unto him in a vision, and will speak unto him in a dream." – Numbers 12:6

All prophets are dreamers but not all dreamers are prophets. God will show you your calling in a dream.

Gideon's victory is sealed in a dream by a Midian solider. *"And when Gideon came behold a man told his fellow a dream, and said, behold I dreamt a dream, and a cake of barley bread tumbled from heaven into the Midian camp and smote it that it fell, and overturned it, that the tent lay along." –* Judges 7:13

Gideon saw his victory and was encouraged because of the dreams he had. Your victory will be sealed even in a dream.

Solomon

"In Gibeon the Lord appeared to Solomon in a dream by night; and God said, ask what I shall give you." – 1 Kings 3:5

Solomon in a dream saw God and had a conversation with Him. God asked him to say whatever he wants. Solomon chose wisdom. God gives Solomon riches and honor.

It's important to see that this happened in a dream. Things that manifest in the physical would have already happened in the spiritual. I encourage you to look and see that God will release a lot of things in dreams that you then experience in the natural. Job explains that God speaks to us in a dream Job 33:14. Jeremiah told people to be careful about wrong prophecies. "The prophet that has a dream let him tell a dream." Nebuchadnezzar saw the future through a dream

*"Daniel dreamed dreams, where with his spirit was troubled and his sleep brake from him." –*Daniel 2: 1

Daniel prayed and asked God what Nebuchadnezzar's dream meant, and then he slept and dreamt. He then interprets the

King's dream. The King saw the future in a dream. The prophet Joel prophesies about dreams in Joel2:28. The wise men from the East are warned in a dream not to return to Herod in Mathew 2:12.

Joseph had an encounter with an angel in dreams and was told to take Mary as his wife.

"But while he thought on these things, behold the angel of the Lord appeared unto him in a dream, saying, Joseph, thou son of David fear not." – Mathew 1:20

Other examples in the new testament where God spoke through dreams

"And being warned of God in a dream" – Mathew 2:12

"But when Herod was dead, behold, and an angel of the Lord appeared in a dream to Joseph in Egypt." – Mathew 2:19

"And being warned in a dream he went to Galilee." – Mathew 2:22

All prophets are dreamers but not all dreamers are prophets. God will show you your calling in a dream

3

SOURCES OF DREAMS

Dreams are of paramount importance depending on your understanding. There are three sources of dreams. And these are as follows:

Firstly, God is the giver of dreams. As we have established already, God speaks a lot through dreams. Dreams are one of God's communication tools to us.

Secondly, the human soul is a source of dreams. The human soul also influences a person's dreams. Every person has different likes, passions and actions. What you are going through determines your dreams.

The devil and demons influence your dreams a lot. The fact that God can enter into your dream world, simply means demons can also enter. So you must understand the source of your dreams.

The spiritual reality in your life will influence your dreams and your dreams influence your natural reality. You should, therefore, be careful whom you share your dreams with. There are dream catchers. These are evil spirits that will catch your dreams and convert them into their pleasure. You will dream great things being released to you but you never possess those things. Joseph told his brothers his dreams and they plot to kill him; they call him the dreamer.

Dream catchers intend to kill your dream before its right time. So don't share your dreams with everybody. Not every dream that you get needs to be interpreted. And not every dream that comes to you is a God-given dream.

There are a lot of things that influence dreams but trust God and pray about it. Daniel asked the King for time to go and pray so he could interpret his dream. Always watch and pray and ask the Holy Spirit to direct you. Dreams can come from God. He uses dreams as a means of communicating with men. There are several other means He can use to communicate and dreams are just one of them.

I proved in the previous chapters that this is God's way preferred way of communication. While men sleep, God will speak to his spirit men as a tripartite being. He is a spirit with a soul and lives in a body (Trichotomaus). A man is Trichotomaus.

Let me distinguish what he consisting of. Spirit: In the human spirit you will find communion, intuition and volition (decision making).

Soul: conscience, emotions, senses (touch, smell, sight, test and hearing), mind (conscious, unconscious, and subconscious thoughts).

Body: this is the flesh and blood.

Paul writes in the book of Romans and says, "Our spirit agrees with the spirit of God that we are the children of God." – Romans 8:16

God communicates with the spirit not the soul or body. When we sleep, our spirit is awake and is communicating with God. Your spirit can communicate with God. Your spirit has receptors of what is communicated from the spiritual realm and you will receive it in your spirit. Paul and says, "I will pray in the spirit and I will pray with understanding."

The soul consists of conscience, thoughts, senses and the mind. As a human being goes about his daily activities, his soul will pick up so many things, consciously or unconsciously. Your problems, excitements, or daily engagements will influence your dreams.

Your soul will make you dream. If you are anxious about something it will affect your peace and it will then affect your dreams.

Demons will also cause you to have dreams of things that may affect your life. If God can put things in your life, the devil can take them away and replace them with his counterfeit. The devil will put problems, tools of witchcraft so that your life will go down. A lot of our problems are demonic and as long as people cannot maintain their deliverance, demons will torment them.

Rules of interpreting your dreams

One of the most important subjects that I took in bible school is hermeneutics, which is the science and art of interpretation. It has several rules that I believe apply to this subject matter. Dreams should be taken as literally as possible. What the dream implies is already revealed and there isn't much hidden in it. This is common with a lot of dreams with voices and angels. Prophetic dreams are usually very direct. Every interpretation should be Christo-centric. The centre of our lives and everything is Christ and when we interpret our dreams, Christ should be the centre, not men; not angels but Christ only.

Every dream and its interpretation cannot and should not contradict the word of God. Once the dream is contradicting the principles of the word of God, then we cannot align it to God. God honors his word above all things. I had a dream a couple of years ago that showed me the reality of the dream world.

I was walking in Chitungwiza, a town outside Harare with two other Pastors. As we walked, I saw some demons coming from heaven, falling like balls of fire. The demons would land and their knees were the same height as the tallest building in the town. I started to rebuke the spirits and the demons would burst up in flames. They then stopped coming down. I found myself in a house confronting the storage woman. The woman looked at me and raised her hand. I was pinned to the wall of the house and couldn't move. I tried to rebuke her in Jesus' name but my voice was muffled. I started interceding in my heart. She then lost her strength and fell.

When I stood up, she was defeated then I heard a voice saying, "You have defeated the queen of the coast for the Southern Africa region, now you must go to West Africa". Suddenly, I had wings and began to sow like an eagle. I saw myself in Zambia and my passport was stamped on the 17th of October I landed there because I felt I tired. I woke up but couldn't understand the dream. Immediately, I felt I had to go to the toilet. For three days, I passed out blood only. What had happened in a dream had affected my health. I remember the last time I felt tired of a lot of things, including my ministry, I was in Zambia and it was the 17th of October. Amazingly, dreams are so powerful.

The spiritual reality in your life will influence your dreams and your dreams influence your natural reality

4

COMMON DREAMS AND THEIR INTERPRETATIONS

Common dreams and their interpretations

I have spent the past years praying to have the ability to interpret dreams like Daniel and Joseph. These are some of the most common dreams in many people's lives. In this chapter, I will help to interpret some of the most common dreams in the biblical perspective

Responding to your dream

The most significant thing you must do is to be able to interpret your dreams and take action. You have to act in response to every dream that you obtain or get from God or that is released by demons into your life. When you don't react, you are still responding. When you dream of something, it's important to analyze it. I recommend writing down all of your dreams which is a key to understanding the future, present and the past. You must respond by rebuking the devil so he may flee away.

Praying or having your spiritual father pray for you is also an alternative. In this book, we will explore the area of negative dreams and how you can respond to them. A lot of people say they don't hear God, when God is speaking to them through dreams. Often, they don't respond to those dreams when God has given them a word. When you ignore your dreams, you make yourself vulnerable to attacks from the enemy.

Dreams of spiritual wives or husbands

These dreams have become so common and have been exposed a lot by televangelists. I come across a lot of people who face this challenge in their lives and I help deliver them from these demonic forces. Demons can be married to someone willingly or unwillingly. The word says a person's enemies shall be those of your household, so people from your family can open doors to the realm of the spirit and allow someone to be inhibited or influenced by spiritual spouses. In many cases, I have discovered that it is relatives who use witchcraft to make money by giving away a person to a spiritual spouse because demons require one.

I have dealt with sad stories of girls who cannot get married and guys who can't marry while experiencing serious financial problems but they don't know why. When I ask them, they say they dream of having sex. People, who experience sexual dreams or getting married to a strange person, must not ignore it because this is a sign of a spiritual spouse unleashed by the enemy. Many people who experience demonic attacks in their lives are faced with these problems:

Failure to find a spouse

Broken relationships

Broken marriages

Excessive period pains

Continuous financial problems

Frustration and life roadblocks

Lack of progress in life

In this case, one needs to deal with this spirit urgently. One cannot allow it to rule over him/her. The word says, "Whosoever the son of God set free is free indeed." You have freedom in Jesus Christ and that freedom comes from knowing who you are in Christ Jesus. Pray against that spirit and divorce yourself from any spiritual marriage. I recommend that you repeat the prayer to remove these rings by faith.

"I break away from any spiritual marriage that I am a part of willingly or unwillingly in Jesus' name.

"I break all demonic covenants that I entered into willingly or unknowingly in Jesus name.

"I remove any spiritual covenant ring that was placed on my fingers and I divorce myself from any spiritual marriage I am in Jesus name.

"I break all demonic altars entered on my behalf and all altars that have my name on it in Jesus name."

The word of the Lord says, "Rebuke the devil and he will flee away." A friend was conducting a deliverance service and the Holy Spirit instructed him to tell everybody to pray for their fingers and by faith remove any spiritual wedding rings. As everybody prayed, several girls fell and started screaming and crying out as demons manifested and left them. They had been married in the spirit, they just didn't know it. This is why many people struggle to get married in the natural; it's because they already are married in the realm of the evil spirit.

Eating in your dreams

As I was growing up, I struggled with these dreams. I would be eating different kinds of foods, not limited to bread and meat. Food signifies fellowship and oneness. Every time I dreamt of eating, I woke up full and wouldn't want to eat anything or wanted to vomit. I also noticed that at the edge of a breakthrough, I would have these dreams often and somehow I would lose my breakthrough.

The scripture says, "We are not unaware of the devil's devices." The devil has devices that he uses to attack us so we can be defeated. Watch and pray. Jesus gives us the parable of a sower who goes to plant his wheat field. In the night, the enemy comes and plants his weeds in the same field. While you sleep, the devil and his agents are planting weeds of failure and problems. What did you eat in the dream that made you full and lose appetite during the day?

I come across many people who have accepted that it is

common and it's normal to eat in dreams. Demons would have been feeding you at night and giving you spiritual demonic food. No wonder all things become hard for you. Usually, people who eat in their dreams face:

Blocked breakthroughs

Sickness which there isn't any cure at all

You have to begin to pray more and grow your spiritual men. If Solomon could identify and receive from God in a dream, you can pray, identify and refuse to receive from demons in your dream as well. It's a sign of spiritual weakness to eat in your dreams. Grow your spirit men. Grow him always that you may walk in power and authority. You must eat the word only, which is the true spiritual food not the devil's counterfeit food that brings you problems and pain.

Pray these prayers if you are always having these dreams:

"In the mighty name of Jesus Christ, I close every doorway being used to feed me in my dreams by demons.

"Everything I have eaten in a dream, I vomit it in the mighty name of Jesus Christ.

"Every tool of the devil that has entered my spirit, soul or body due to food I have eaten in a dream, I vomit you right now in the mighty name of Jesus Christ."

Continue to do these prayers and add your own words as you

pray for your deliverance. If the problem persists I recommend that you find a deliverance minister who will pray and deliver you.

Falling hair/shaved head

One can wake up in the morning and discover that their head has been partly shaved. This is common to some people. I will take you to the word of God and what it says about the hair.

"But if a woman has long hair it is a glory to her for her hair is given her for covering." – 1 Corinthians 11:15.

You have to understand that hair talks of power, glory and covering. Samson's hair was a sign of power and authority. His strength was in the hair on the head and thus hair is a sign of power and glory and so when one loses hair, they lose strength and glory. It's a sign of falling from a position of power. The prophet Elisha cursed children that called him bald head because it meant being barren and unproductive. Losing hair is a prophetic sign of strength being lost. Refuse this and pray against it. Some people have lost positions and jobs after losing their hair.

If you are having such dreams, repeat this prayer:

"Every demonic plan to destroy me and expose me is destroyed in the mighty name of Jesus Christ.

"Every demon put in my path to steal my glory, must fall and die in Jesus' name.

"Every monitoring spirit monitoring my life and progress be exposed and destroyed in Jesus' name."

Falling Teeth

I spoke to many people in my family and I realized that dreams of falling teeth, coming off or breaking off of teeth was common. What you need to understand is that teeth reveal aging. Your age is revealed by the number or type of teeth in your mouth. Therefore, losing teeth is a sign of a shortened life. Whenever you dream of losing teeth, you are losing years in your life. I noticed that all first born children in my family, from my great grandfather, my grandfather, my father, and my eldest brother, died before they reached fifty years. We have begun to pray against this in our family and we have seen God change that. Pray that years of fruitfulness may be added to you and not removed.

"Every spirit of death, sickness and untimely death I break your hold over my life.

"Every demonic covenant entered on my behalf by demons and spirits is destroyed in the mighty name of Jesus Christ."

Nakedness in a dream

Nakedness is a sign of a spirit of shame. The first mention of the word naked was with Adam and Eve in Genesis 2:25. Shame was only dealt with by being given a covering. Every time someone received a coat (covering) in the bible, it was a sign of an anointing that was coming upon him. Joseph first receives a coat in his father's house then another in Potiphar's house and finally as the Prime Minister of Egypt. A coat speaks of covering, anointing and authority and when you are without one, then you are naked; you are open and vulnerable to attacks. Pray for the covering of the blood of Jesus. Pray that God can cover you completely with His blood. Don't be vulnerable to attacks from the enemy. A solder is known by his clothing, his covering determines who he is. Pray against the spirit of nakedness in your life.

"I declare my covering in the blood of Jesus Christ. I declare I am a tither and my life, property and finances are covered in the blood of Jesus Christ."

Chased in dreams

Many people we took through deliverance were being chased by headless bodies (demons), dogs (territorial spirits) and sometimes by police or sexual demons. These dreams are a sign of a spirit pursuing you.

"But the Egyptians pursued after them, all the horses and chariots of Pharaoh." – Exodus 14:9

This is a sign of a demonic manifestation of spirits that are after you. Many families have been dedicated to demons and familiar spirits that are after them. I remember reading a book by Dr Olokuya entitled: When the Delivered Needs Deliverance. Many who are Christians still struggle with failure, broken marriages, and failure in business. They are being chased by spirits that follow families. Some demons may have been in a family for generations and they follow individuals for years. What the father did, a child may do the same. The word says, "I will visit the sins of the fathers upon the children to the third and fourth generation." You have to deal with the sins and the iniquities of your father so that you don't go through exactly what they went through. Pray for blindness to all demons that follow you through your bloodline.

"I declare that I am the righteousness of God and no demon shall chase me and have authority over my life.

"I declare I have the DNA of God because everyone that received Christ is a child of God and the bible says all that received him, he gave them the power to be the children of God.

"I speak blindness to all demons and spirits that follow me in Jesus name."

Snakes spirits

A snake is referred to as a serpent in the bible and it's the first figurative animal to represent the devil in the scriptures.

"Now the serpent was more subtle than any beast of the field which the Lord God had made." – Genesis 3: 1

Psalms 140:3 and Psalms 13:3.

The word serpent is nachash in Hebrew which is figuratively

the practice of divination and fortune telling. I have taken many people through deliverance who were troubled by snake spirits. The devil is revealed in the Garden of Eden as a serpent or a snake. Snakes are subtle, dangerous and can kill you. Snakes around bodies, especially around girls' waists, cause them to have unusual sexual appetite and usually close to prostitution.

Snakes have a lot to do with witchcraft, Satanism and extremely dangerous demonic powers that can control a person's life.

I once prayed for someone who dreamt of snakes. As I prayed for Samantha (name changed), she fell and began to slither like a snake. When I rebuked the spirit, she confessed that she always dreamt of snakes everywhere and around her waist. She had been sexually active from a young age and she couldn't go for a day without sex. Anything which is done by compulsion and addiction is demonic. Thank God she was set free. The devil is called the serpent and no snake dream is a good dream. The bible says, "Thou shall trample upon snakes and scorpions." You have to take action against snake and scorpion dreams. Take action and take action now. Fast and pray a lot before you sleep.

Scorpions

Scorpions are spirits of pain. They bring pain to the human body. You need to identify them. Every time a scorpion is present in your dreams, you should realize that you have been attacked by the spirit of pain, sickness or a broken heart will follow immediately after such a dream. Quickly identify them and pray against it.

"Son of man, I am sending you to the Israelites, to a rebellious nation that has rebelled against me; they and their fathers have been in revolt against me to this very day. The people to whom I am sending you are obstinate and stubborn. Say to them, 'This is what the Sovereign Lord says."

"And whether they listen or fail to listen — for they are a rebellious house — they will know that a prophet has been among them. And you, son of man, do not be afraid of them or their words. Do not be afraid, though briers and thorns are all around you and you live among scorpions. Do not be afraid of what they say or terrified by them, though they are a rebellious house." – Ezekiel 2:3-6

The most significant thing you must do is to be able to interpret your dreams and take action

5

ANIMALS IN DREAMS

Animals in dreams

In the African culture, especially in Bantu tribes, people identify which clan or tribe one belongs to through the association of animals. What you need to understand is that men were given power over animals but then he has lowered himself to a position of identifying himself with animals that were created by God. What is greater, a man or animals? Animals have minds but no they have no spirit that can be inhabited by demons as in the case of the pigs that received thousands of spirits from Legion. You cannot, therefore, associate yourself with an animal for you were given dominion over all things on earth, in the air and under the sea.

Dogs

In the Israelite culture, dogs were treated with contempt, and figuratively, temple male prostitutes were called dogs. Anything unwanted was thrown to the dogs. Exodus 22:31. Even when you sold your dog, you could not bring the offering or tithe to the house of the Lord, according to Deuteronomy 23:18.

"For dogs have compassed me: the assembly of the wicked has enclosed me: they pierced my hands and my feet." – Psalms 22:16

"Deliver me from the sword; my precious life from the power of the dog." – Psalms 22:20

"At night they return like howling dogs; they prowl around the city." – Psalms 59:6

"Beware of dogs, beware of evil workers." – Philippians 3:2

In all cases I have dealt with anyone bitten by a dog in a dream, they will either have a sickness or are in serious problems. Dogs, therefore, symbolize territorial spirits.

Lions

These are animals of great strength and are territorial animals too. I have come to understand that every time there are serious problems in a person's life, these are the spirits that usually appear in dreams.

"Look! The people are like Lions. Like the Lion, he rises up! He does not lie down again until he has consumed his prey and drunk the blood of the slain." –

Numbers 23:24

"No lions will be there no nor will any ferocious beasts get up on it, and they will not be found there. But the redeemed will walk there." – Isaiah 35:9

Pray against lion dreams, which symbolize spirit mediums in the African Traditional Religion (ATR).

Baboons

These are spirits of poverty. Baboons pick the crumbs and move in troops. The proverb says "And poverty shall attack you." It's a serious attack by the spirit of poverty. Pray against it but also tithe and sow into the Kingdom. You can classify all these animals as beasts, whether they are tamed or wild because they represent spiritual attacks.

Donkeys

These are beasts of burden but also very stubborn. Dreams of donkeys depended on the context usual but usually speak of a stubborn situation that resists change.

Bats

These signify life in darkness and desolate places. It's a sign of spirits that lurk in darkness and desolate places and may imply that you are going through a dark period in your life.

Birds

Birds are creatures of the sky in the realm of the spirit. Birds are well symbolized in the bible and it makes their interpretation easier and more accessible. Generally, birds are demons and you see it in several dreams. Joseph's interpretation of the baker's dream, birds ate out of the basket which was on his head. So birds symbolize the spirit of death. Jesus gives out a parable.

"And when he sowed, some seed fell by the way side and the fowls came and devoured them up." – Mathew 13:3

In the parable, birds of the air, which are demons, ate up the word. In Joseph's case, the birds ate bread off the baker's head. Bread is the gospel; it's God's word. Birds symbolize thieves who will steal your future, your seed, and your wealth. They should die in Jesus name.

A friend was approached by a woman who dreamt of a hen with six chicks that had just hatched but a big bird took away one. When she woke up, she never bothered to enquire about the dream; she thought it only referred to natural chickens. Before the day was over, one of her six children died mysteriously. He was the only boy. If shad watched and seen what the dream was saying, she should have seen it coming and prayed against it. Don't take dreams lightly; it may make the difference between life and death. God is still speaking; listen carefully to every dream and spiritual reality. The bible says God does nothing without first revealing it to His prophets and servants. Watch out especially for many birds, vultures, crows, and all kinds of birds of prey.

Doves

They are a symbol of the Holy Spirit, love, and peace.

Turtle doves

They are also a symbol of peace.

Eagles

These birds symbolize Christians, the prophetic and victorious spiritual life. – Job 39:27-30

Vultures

These birds are a symbol of the scavenging spirits. They are known to circle a dying or a dead animal. Each time these birds appear there is a spirit of death around it. They are also a symbol of fake or false prophets. – Leviticus 11:14, Deuteronomy 14:13 and Job 28:7

Bees

Bees signify a spiritual attack by an army of demons. This dream shows that a major spiritual attack is coming.

"They compassed me about like bees; they are quenched as the fire of thorns." – Psalms 118:12

It's important to pray against these kinds of attacks. When you dream bees stinging you, this will be a sign that demonic poison has been released into your system. Bees are producers of honey but at the same time can have a fatal bite.

Pigs

Pigs are a sign of unclean spirits that do not respect good and precious things. – Psalms 80:13

Worms

These are found in decaying things. They, therefore, represent death or dying things. It may be the death of a relationship or even a business. – Exodus 16:24, Isaiah 14:11 and Job 7:5

Chameleons

These creatures change color depending on where they are. They camouflage themselves wherever they are; therefore it's a symbol of fake people who are not revealing who they are.

Elephants

These are territorial spirits.

Grasshoppers

This is a spirit of the devourer

Horses

These are animals of war that also symbolizes Angelic beings.

Lambs

A sign of humility and also a sign of Christ or the believer

Rat

It's a symbol of the spirit of destruction.

Peacock

A symbol of the spirit of pride, – 1Kings 10:22

Spiders

Job 8:14

Life cut short in dreams

Many people have been warned in dreams to watch out for attacks but never took them seriously. If a person can be attacked with a knife or a gun in a dream, they are facing demonic powers. A lot of sicknesses that have no cure, even miscarriages are a result of demonic shots with knives, arrows, and guns from the enemy in a dream. If you notice that all vices including prostitution, drug abuse, murder, rape and witchcraft happen at night. Why? Night time is when hell is unleashed on earth. Pray against all demonic attacks.

"For we wrestle not against flesh and blood but against principalities and against powers, against rulers of the darkness of this world, against spiritual wickedness in high places Wherefore take unto you the whole armor of God that you may be able to withstand in the evil day." – Ephesians 6:12b

Roadblocks

I spoke to someone who always dreamt of policemen. All the time he begins to progress, he would dream of policemen or soldiers around him. You must watch out for demonic police and soldiers who mount roadblocks over you and close every avenue towards your success. Pray against the spirit of being nearly but every time you are about to receive your miracle, something shows up. Pray against the spirit of failure at the edge of your miracle. These may come as dreams of doors closing just before you enter; this is the spirit of blockage.

Retrogressive spirits

This is usually shown in a dream when one is a child, in a uniform or writing an examination, and always failing to complete the exam. You can deal with this spirit and begin to live a fruitful life. I have spoken to many people and prayed for those who do everything but they aren't progressing at all. If there is no progression in your life, this is due to these spirits. Until you deal with this demon of retrogression, your life will border on failure and no achievements at all.

If you are one of the people who face this demon, begin to declare the word of God over your life:

"I am the head and not the tail. I am blessed I am not cursed. I am the righteousness of God. I am going to the next level."

Marine spirits

The majority of people I have taken through deliverance were under attack from marine demons. Marine demons are associated with the water world. Some had the demons come into them by opening doors after consulting sangomas (witch doctors) or some white garment churches that use water or pebbles for deliverance. You must know that the water world is real. I have spoken to ex-Satanists, who confess of having been into the water world, under the seas with mermaids. One girl I spoke to said she had a dream and mermaids said they control prostitution and fashion, among other things. Many, who dream of water, don't know its symbolism.

Let's explore the good and the bad.

Rain

Dreams of rain usually symbolize showers of blessing.

River

A place to the next level, for example, the Jordan was the place of crossing over. It's an important dream of crossing over a bridge to the other side.

Mist

Covering, – Genesis 2:6

Dew

Watering, – Genesis 27:27

Well

A place of generational blessings, – Psalms 84:6; Genesis 26:18

Clouds

God's presence and movement, – Psalms 9:13; 1Cor 10:1

Sea

A place of testing and now dimension

Swimming

This is a sign of attack by marine spirits in your life

Walking in water

This is a sign that you are under the authority of marine demons.

Walking on top of the water/bridge

You have crossed over. – Psalms 6:6

Fishing with your feet in the water

You have the power of wealth but marine spirits are stealing from you.

Dirty water

There shows marine spirit attacks in your life, usually, an accusation is coming against you.

Mermaids

The queen of the coast/princess of Satan has arisen against you. You may have been initiated into Satanism unaware, usually, through gifts, you receive like jeweler, money, food, or clothing. You should be careful who gives you presents and pray for whatsoever you receive. Water leaking into your house is a sign of an open door in your life and demons are leaking problems into your life. Water is also a sign of the stagnation of the Holy Spirit in your life.

Flies

These are a symbol of death as these follow dead things.

Frogs

It's a symbol of a spirit of instability.

Hail storms

A destructive judgment has been issued against you.

Swimming

If you always have a dream swimming in an open sea, it's probably that you were initiated into Satanism or witchcraft and you must seek deliverance. A friend once prayed for a girl who always loved to be in the water. If she went to take a bath, she would spend at least an hour. If she went swimming, she would do 3 to 5 hours and she always swam in her dreams. When she was prayed for, she manifested some serious marine demons. – Exodus 9:23-25

Some people smell like fish, even after applying deodorants. This is a sign of the presence of marine spirits. In most parts of the world, some people use these spirits for fishing but whoever eats the fish will find it tasteless because the spirits would have fed on the fish's blood first. Every time spirit mediums are possessed by a spirit, they ask for water. This is because water is a medium to another world and it will cool them down after crossing the chasm from hell to earth. Never give someone you are taking through deliverance water if they ask for it.

A couple of years ago, a deliverance team had finished the day's service, praying and casting out many demons. When they got home, they were given food. They washed their hands and after the meal, a small girl was asked to pour out the water used by the deliverance team. As she did, she fell without the Elder's knowledge. Her mother waited for some minutes but the child didn't return. She went outside and saw the child lying motionless on the ground. She brought her to the Pastor, who prayed for her and after a few minutes, the demons manifested. They said they had been in the hands of the Pastors and had gone into the water and later entered the child as she was about to throw the dirty water away.

I imagine how many products like hair weaves, the so-called 100 percent human hair, food, water, and juices that are carrying demons in them. "We are not unaware of the devil's devices." Marine spirits have caused a lot of problems as they control music, fashion, entertainment, sicknesses, abortions, and divorces. Unfortunately, we are unaware of these spirits even though they are there. We walk with them, live with them; yet they destroy marriages churches, families, and businesses. There are millions of people under their influence. I wish the church of Jesus Christ would wake up from its slumber and fight these demons.

Problems associated with marine spirits

Prostitution, homosexuality, sicknesses without cure, unexplained uncontrollable deaths, and rage, Fight these demons and pray against them, you are more than a conqueror.

Dreams of struggle in life, poverty, and debt

Someone once wrote to me and said that "I am praying for you that you may come to a place where you don't have issues at all." I believe there is a place like that. I believe you can get there; it is possible to live life as God intended it. I pray that you may have life and have it more abundantly. You can have the God kind of life; the ZOE, the effervescent, and the bubbling kind of life. It's possible. I didn't live it, till I started to believe that it's possible.

Now let me take you through some dreams that show signs of struggle.

Dreams of spending money lavishly, buying and barefoot

Dreams of torn shoes

Dreams of you wearing rags

Dreams of old coins and notes

Dreams of always struggling

Thieves stealing from you in a dream

Falling from a high building but can't reach the bottom

Leaking wallet/pocket

Losing money and not finding it

Dreams of struggling to climb a mountain

Travelling an endless journey in a dream, meaning an unprofitable endeavor

All these dreams are a sign of struggling. It may be in marriage, finances, ministry, or life in general.

I encourage you to begin to fill yourself with these words

"By thy words, thou shall be justified and by thy words though shall be condemned." – Matthew 12:37

"For I say unto you who so ever shall say unto this mountain be thou be removed it shall be so." – Mark 11:23

The best way to deal with poverty is in two ways: prayer and giving. The poor need to give to get themselves out of poverty. If you cannot give yourself, you will die in poverty. The bible says, "Give and it shall be given back to you good measure, pressed down and shaken together shall man give to you." – Luke 6:38

Don't worry about your portion; you can have whatever you desire. When the counsel of wickedness arises against you, some people will dream people, who will be accusing them or surrounded by dead people accusing them. At one time, my spiritual father said, "Brian there is a conspiracy in the heavens against you. Be careful because your enemy will plan and plot against you. In some of the dreams, you will see people seated in a circle or half-moon position and they are talking about you. It is a counsel of wickedness." Pray that all counsel of wickedness assigned against you may fall and fail in Jesus name.

Dreams of dead people

The word of God says, "The dead shall not have anything to do with the living." The dead are now in their realm and the living on their own. And as such, we do not meet. Demons that come into people's lives wearing the faces of dead relatives show a lack of closure and acceptance of the loss of a relative and this will open up doors for the demons to come in as those dead relatives. Familiar spirits have also taken advantage of these situations and come into people's lives and they have been accepted. These spirits of death will kill everything in your life, either in marriage, business or ministry.

Spiritual attacks

You will see these through dreams of bees and rats. Bees are a sign of spiritual attack coming into your life and it may be on your health or any other area. The rats are a sign of attack on your finances. Rats show the spirit of the devourer and the devourer will destroy your wealth and your finances. Even if you see the rat in a dream or the natural in your house it shows the spirit of the devourer. Rebuke the devil and he will flee away.

Colors

Colors are symbolic of many things.

We should be able to identify the different colors even in a dream. There are different colors that we will look at

Purple is for royalty

Yellow for prophecy

Gold for wealth

Green for life

White for purity

Black for sin/death

Until you deal with this demon of retrogression, your life will border on failure and no achievements at all.

UNDERSTANDING AND INTERPRETING DREAMS

6

GODLY DREAMS

Numbers

Numbers are important in life and especially in dreams. Numbers are usually the last thing people notice in a dream. Pharaoh dreams of seven fat and seven lean cows. These represented seven years each. So numbers are important in interpreting a dream. The baker dreamt three baskets on top of his head and this turned out to be three days. Watch out for these things. Some hermeneutical interpretations of numbers are as follows:

1 is the number of God/oneness

2 is the number of witnesses

3 is the number of testimony

4 is the number of the world

5 is the number of grace

6 is the number of human order

7 number of perfection and completion

8 is the number of a new beginning

9 is the number of rebirth or giving birth

10 is the number of human government and order

11 is the number of disintegration and transition

12 is the number of government and order

40 is the number of testing and conquering

A couple of months ago, I had a dream where I was standing with three different men of God; a Bishop, an Apostle, and a Prophet. This dream was powerful and as I interpreted the dream, it was the same with Jesus' transfiguration. It was a confirmation of my calling and gifting. Therefore, there was a fullness of testimony with three of the world greatest gifts standing with me. That was a very significant dream. At least five people, the number of grace have experienced the same dream in our church. They saw the church has grown so much. Multitudes were attending our service. We are claiming this currently.

Feelings

You can dream of being at a party or being at a wedding but you have a feeling of things that things are not well. This feeling will linger around you the whole day. Never ignore those feelings. Do not take lightly the feelings you will have in a dream. The feelings may be more important than the word and event in a dream; don't take anything lightly.

You aren't supposed to have feelings in a dream but when you have those feelings; it's important to note them because they tell you a lot of things.

Voices in dreams

Several times, I have dreamt and hearing voices in my dreams as if someone was speaking but I never saw the person. This is common when God is sending a specific message to you. The voice has helped me take the right direction in life so many times. Biblically, Samuel was called during the night three times. He hears a voice but doesn't see the speaker. Moses saw a burning bush, heard a voice, and never saw the speaker. God will speak and you will not see the speaker. It's often likely in those dreams that God is speaking to you.

Men of God

Each time God wants to rebuke me, I see a famous prophet in a dream and he will give me the message. Whenever it's a dream that has something to do with ministry, I see my spiritual father coming to speak to me. Many people that I spoke to, have had the same dream in their life. You should be able to notice the person that was in the dream and what gifting do they have? Is it Apostolic, Prophetic or Pastoral, and what message are they bringing to you?

The most important thing to remember is that an angel will appear wearing the face of a man of God. A few years ago, I had a dream where my Bishop walked into the church as I was about to preach. I noticed that there were two Pastors in the crowd famous, who are famous in the country. My Bishop then asked me in the dream what these two were doing in my church. He told me in the dream not to associate with these two at all. Months later, I understood the dream. When God sends angels like that; it's a very important message.

Angels

The challenge with angels is that they appear differently to different people. "Some have entertained angels unknowingly." So it's easy to meet an angel and not recognize it. The same is also true of dreams. You will see angels and not even recognize them. They do appear with messages, some as children some as adults, and they will help you in a dream by giving you a message. Be on the lookout in your dream for angels. Pray that the spiritual men is alert to the presence of angels in your dream world

Killing snakes/animals, deliverance

The Holy Spirit has taken a lot of people through deliverance as they sleep. At times demons appear as snakes, clay pots, dogs, and other animals. You will fight against these animals and you will prevail against them. This is a sign of progress in your life. As you kill these things in your dreams, you are defeating demons that steal your breakthrough and miracles. You will find your spirit fighting battles and waging wars on your behalf. Things will be revealed; where and what has been put into your life by the enemy. I have heard people tell me of dreams where they killed snakes or rats which were in the house and the following morning they found dead rats or snakes. The power at work in dreams is the spirit of the devourer; fight it. Be conscious of what you are fighting in your dreams and prevail over it.

Vomit in a dream

Several people have had these kinds of dreams. Some vomit the most disgusting things such as feces or meat. The devil is very cunning and will at times in deposit into a person's body tools of witchcraft, failure, and all kinds of marks that will make the demons have access to your life. Some people eat in dreams or just have blotted tummies because of eating in their dreams. These dreams produce problems and hindrances of all kinds in one's life. The Holy Spirit in Jesus Christ name will bring deliverance. Some people will vomit or will have things coming out of their mouths. At times, they will see someone removing things from their bodies. Praise the Lord for your deliverance.

Do not take lightly the feelings you will have in a dream. The feelings may be more important than the word and event in a dream; don't take anything lightly.

75

7

BREAKTHROUGH DREAMS

Rain

Of all water dreams, rain is the safe dream and it has nothing to do with marine spirits. Rain is a sign of spiritual blessing coming upon you. Rain is pure and therefore a sign of blessing. Other forms of water are:

Well

It is a place of generational blessings. All the significant people in the bible found a wife at a well.

River

It is the place of the next level. Jesus is baptized in the Jordan River. Namman was healed in a river. Elijah was taken to heaven at the Jordan River. And Israel crossed into the Promised Land at the Jordan River.

Sea

It is a place of crossing over.

Bridges

This seems to be a common dream for many people. The dreams come while one is walking and they come to a big river or a sea they have to cross over. Usually, they don't know how they will do it. They will look around and suddenly they see a bridge to cross over or they walk on top of the water and they cross over. This dream talks of supernatural provision that will take you to the next level of your life, ministry, or business.

When God provides a means to cross over to the other side, it will be established. Whatever situation you are facing, if you came across this dream, you will have a breakthrough.

Singing and praying in a dream

I love these kinds of dreams; they take to lift you spiritually. These dreams will make you walk in power. A lot of people have sung with angels in their dreams. Some have prayed and woke up in the morning still praying. This is a sign of your spirit men engaging in battle on your behalf. You thought you are sleeping but your spirit man is fully awake. I have met people who speak in tongues in their dreams but not in the natural. It is because your spirit received the gift but it is yet to manifest in the natural. You have to work on the flesh to pull down the barrier to receive it.

Wealth in a dream

Dreams of money, usually lots of it and dreams of precious stones signify that wealth has been released into your life. If you dream about this, and you still are in poverty; it's a sign that the enemy has stolen your wealth. Claim it back! I used to dream of driving a car, holding a precious stone in my hand. A certain man would always come and take it away, driving off in my car. This was a sign of manipulation and control over my life and wealth through witchcraft. Do not let the enemy take your wealth. When you receive money in a dream, wake up, and claim it. You are blessed and not cursed. You are rich through Christ Jesus.

Repeated dreams

It's important to take note of repeated dreams. God will speak twice or thrice so that you can understand that it is important and significant. Do not take lightly a dream that comes more than once lightly.

"God speaks once, twice yet man does not perceive it." – Job 33:14.

When a dream is repeated, always seek interpretation.

Driving in a dream

I have met people who had this dream many times. Driving a bus in most cases has something to do with ministry or business. Driving a car has something to do with your personal life; it must be you driving not someone else. Usually, if someone driving your car, there is manipulation and control of your life and destiny don't allow it.

Your call to ministry

I have identified gifted people who have risen to significance after a dream. The first dream is preaching. A lot of people see themselves preaching. Some see themselves standing before crowds and this is extremely significant. Some people receive a transfer of power or anointing by receiving a rod or a coat in a dream. Your gift or calling is usually confirmed in a dream. I have dreamt preaching, casting out demons, and healing the sick in a dream many times. Your dreams will confirm and affirm your ministerial calling. In these particular dreams, notice exactly what you are doing because it will point to your future calling.

Other interpretations in brief

An airplane represents a large ministry

An alligator/crocodile represent a leviathan spirit; a demon

A bald head represents shame/lost glory

Bathing symbolizes a problem with the soul and need for cleansing

A bathroom is a place of cleaning or dealing with emotional issues

Your gift or calling is usually confirmed in a dream

8

SETTING CAPTIVES FREE

Open doors

"If you do well shall you not be accepted but you shall not do well sin lies at the door and its desire is for you." – Genesis 4:7

The devil can never operate in anyone's life without authorization. What the enemy needs is legal ground or a legal right and he will start to operate in your life. Proverbs says, "A curse without a cause will not come." Whenever you find the enemy operating in your life, there is an open door somewhere. Exodus 20:5 says, "I will visit the iniquities of the fathers upon the sons up until the fourth generation." There is nothing that just happens. Something somewhere has triggered the enemy to operate in your life.

"When Jesus saw him in the temple he said behold thou has been made whole sin no more least a worst thing came upon thee." – John 5:14

Spiritual doors that open in your life will cause demonic princes and powers to enter, bringing problems into your life. These doors open because of sin. Therefore sin will make you vulnerable to demonic attack. The word of God encourages us not to fall into sin. If we do, we should confess and forsake our sins. Do not allow any sin to remain in your life. Note that also our families open legal ground for the enemy to bring backlash over us through things like:

Consulting spirit mediums

Consulting sangomas or witch doctors

Involvement with witches and wizards

Horoscopes and new age religion

Involvement with white garment churches

Occultism and involvement with cults

Gifts from satanic agents

Dedication to family and demonic alters

There are also personal doors that one can open through:

Music

Pornography

Sexual immorality

Unforgiving

Watching horror movies

Other religions, especially ones use ungodly meditation

I encourage you to renounce, confess, and turn away from sin for God is faithful and just to forgive you, no matter what sin you are into; God can take you out of it. It does not matter what it is. You can be forgiven and set free. Identify the sins of your family, confess them and pray these prayers

"Lord I confess the sin of... which was committed by me or my family. Today, I commit to forsake it and I cover myself with the blood of Jesus Christ. From this day forth, every door which was opened because of this sin, I close it down. Every demon which came into my life as a result of this open door, I cast it out of my life right now in Jesus' name. Amen!"

At times you will yawn or tears will come out as you say this prayer and deliverance will be taking place.

He came to set the captives free

You cannot as a Christian live under the bondage and slavery of the devil. You can breakthrough whatever the enemy puts in your path. It doesn't matter what the devil throws at you, you can overcome. The word of God says, "We are more than conquerors through Christ Jesus." It means we have already won. The book of Colossians says, "Jesus Christ conquered all powers and principalities and made a public demonstration triumphing over them. Jesus Christ has already overpowered them." As the bible says, "we are now seated with Jesus Christ in heavenly places." You are a child of God and can overcome anything, do not be afraid or live as a scared Christian. Jesus Christ has already set you free

I encourage you to do the following prayers and declarations:

"Everything I have eaten and consumed in a dream I destroy it by the fire of the Holy Ghost. Every dream that the enemy has taken away from me I take it back in Jesus name.

"Every demonic thief stealing money, wealth, and breakthrough in dreams, I burn you by fire in Jesus name. Everything I have eaten in a dream I vomit it now in the name of Jesus.

"Every open door in my life that is allowing the enemy to have authority over me through dreams, I close you by the power of the blood of Jesus Christ."

I encourage you to take all dreams seriously, they may have more implications than you realize. We often ignore dreams that will eventually huge implications in our lives. We usually live to regret, having not watched, listened, and given heed to the dreams that we had.

Thank you for reading this book and we pray you were been blessed.

For feedback, sales and bookings please contact our offices: +263774742747

Email: bmgabazi@gmail.com

ABOUT THE AUTHOR

Brian Mgabazi serves as the Presiding Bishop of Covenant Life Ministries International which incorporates Covenant Life Churches, Covenant Faith Churches South Africa, Covenant Life Ministries Botswana and Igreja Nova Vida Alianca Mozambique, Covenant Life Bible Institute, Brian Mgabazi Apostolic Network and Heal Africa Trust. He is also the founding President of Apostolic Bishops Network which is an association of Apostles and Bishops. He has been in Ministry for since 1999 and been preaching since 1989. He is a renowned conference speaker especially on leadership, Kingdom Order, Kingdom structures and Kingdom Strategies.

www.ingramcontent.com/pod-product-compliance
Lightning Source LLC
Chambersburg PA
CBHW061429050726
47593CB00006B/2265